ENGINEERING
AND BUILDING ROBOTS FOR
COMPETITIONS

MARGAUX BAUM AND JOEL CHAFFEE

New York

Published in 2018 by The Rosen Publishing Group, Inc.
29 East 21st Street, New York, NY 10010

First Edition

Library of Congress Cataloging-in-Publication Data

Names: Baum, Margaux, author. | Chaffee, Joel, author.
Title: Engineering and building robots for competitions / Margaux Baum and Joel Chaffee.
Description: New York : Rosen Publishing, 2018. | Series: Hands-on robotics | Includes bibliographical references and index. | Audience: Grades 5–8.
Identifiers: LCCN 2017026402| ISBN 9781499438871 (library bound) | ISBN 9781499438840 (pbk.) | ISBN 9781499438857 (6 pack)
Subjects: LCSH: Mobile robots—Competitions—Juvenile literature. | Robots—Design and construction—Juvenile literature.
Classification: LCC TJ211.415 .B38 2018 | DDC 629.8/92—dc23
LC record available at https://lccn.loc.gov/2017026402

Manufactured in China

CONTENTS

INTRODUCTION 4

CHAPTER ONE
PICKING A COMPETITION 7

CHAPTER TWO
BUILD A TEAM I3

CHAPTER THREE
DESIGN AND CONSTRUCT I9

CHAPTER FOUR
BUILD YOUR ROBOT 25

CHAPTER FIVE
GO HEAD-TO-HEAD 33

GLOSSARY 39
FOR MORE INFORMATION 4I
FOR FURTHER READING 43
BIBLIOGRAPHY 44
INDEX 46

INTRODUCTION

Robotics competitions have become more popular than ever before, both within the United States and internationally. Once a pursuit for fringe hobbyists, robotics clubs and leagues now exist all over and are sanctioned and sponsored by schools at all levels (elementary, intermediate, and high school), colleges and universities, local organizations and trade groups, and technology organizations and associations, including many entities in the private sector. Besides being great fun, they also help incubate the next generation of roboticists, many of whom go on to higher education and employment in this expanding and important industry.

Such competitions are so widespread that young enthusiasts (and their clubs) have many to choose from. All competitions bring their inventors' robotic creations head-to-head for challenges and contests. However, the rules, qualification criteria, focus, and many other parameters differ greatly among various competitions. Some are regional, others national or international in scope.

While technical know-how and skills in science, technology, engineering, and math (STEM) are obviously incredibly important pillars of a winning robot, a robotics competition also requires good teamwork, time management, and many other factors. Members of a technically superior team might not finish their project on time or be able to come together as a group to meet crucial milestones. Sometimes all it takes is one good idea and the ability to follow through on it.

Team members who band together for competitions have to be able to deal with stress and learn from mistakes, employing a trial-and-error approach, rather than being complete perfectionists. They must be flexible instead of rigid.

Robots fill the venue floor during the FIRST Robotics Competition held at Boston University's Agganis Arena in April 2011. The competition featured teams from in and around Boston and greater New England.

Many of the elements that go into successful showings in robotics competitions need to be in place long before a team fields robots in the actual contests. These include making sure to set up a club or competition team in ways that maximize everyone's skills. Someone might be the best at bringing in and spending money. Another member might be best at leading the team, while others are most proficient at designing and building the actual robots.

Of course, winning competitions is the ultimate goal, and it can definitely feel great to win. But participating in robotics competitions helps young people in many ways. Participants build their technical skills and learn how to work in teams and on deadlines. Competitors at all levels can network with local robotics professionals and even influential members of groundbreaking robotics companies at the higher levels. They can make contacts that will help them in their educations and careers, gain mentors, and make lifelong friends. All in all, engineering and building robots for competition is great for those who try their hardest and are eager to learn.

CHAPTER ONE

PICKING A COMPETITION

There are many different kinds of robotics competitions out there. Many limit their contests to all-student teams, though some are less stringent. A great majority of competitions are geared toward a particular age group or level of schooling—for example, only freshmen and sophomores in high school, or only college-level pupils. Others are only open to school-based teams in particular regions, or even skill-set levels. Before you or

Some robotics clubs take root in technology or engineering classes that college students, high schoolers, and even younger students are enrolled in.

your club or team sets its sights on entering a particular contest, it is vital to research it and its sponsors thoroughly, so as not to waste your time or that of the sanctioning bodies or sponsors.

THE BASICS OF COMPETITION

The competition needs to be far enough in advance for proper preparation of the robot. Preparation might take a while and may go over deadline, a fact that all clubs must keep in mind. Think about how much time can realistically be allocated to the goal. When in doubt, be conservative about the estimate, and if it seems there will not be enough time to prepare, there probably won't be. Competition winners choose competitions that allow time for building and testing.

Indoor arenas and outdoor tracks are not the only competition venues. A member of the robotics club at Jesuit High School in Sacramento, California, resets equipment while testing an aquatic robot.

If one is in the competition to win it (and who isn't?), then it is a good idea to examine what the winnings are. Is there a prize, and what is it? Sometimes the prize is cash that winners may spend however they like. At other times the prize is something else, like a scholarship, a job, a piece of equipment, or money toward a future project. Sometimes it is a combination of the two; but it can also be simply prestige in the robot-building community, and there may be no actual material prize.

How much money can be spent on the project is very important and will determine how competitive the project can realistically be. One may be a serious enthusiast and willing to back knowledge and expertise with a reasonable sum of money from private or family sources, but for some types of

TECHNICAL HIGH SCHOOLS: RIPE FOR ROBOTICS COMPETITIONS

Many high schools field robotics teams. For example, Mountain Home High School of Mountain Home, Arkansas, is home to a robotics team, the Baxter Bomb Squad. It is affiliated with the FIRST Robotics Competition (For Inspiration and Recognition of Science and Technology), one of the most well-known and prolific sponsors of robotics challenges in the United States and abroad. In 2015, local paper *Baxter Bulletin* reported that the team celebrated its twentieth year building robots for FIRST. The team is jointly supported by the high school itself and the local Baxter Healthcare Corporation. Such partnerships commonly work together to fund robotics teams all over.

competitions one's personal resources simply won't have a chance against those backed by a large institutional sponsor, such as a university.

If one is looking to win the DARPA challenge (currently consisting of building a vehicle capable of navigating an urban environment) and grab the $2 million prize, it will require facing teams from Stanford, the Massachusetts Institute of Technology (MIT), and the like, with nearly limitless budgets. And some components, such as sensors, microcontrollers, and such, simply cost money and cannot be improvised. Realizing this early on and focusing effort on competitions that can realistically be won, given the budget, is a very smart decision to make that can save plenty of frustration and disappointment later on.

VARIETIES OF COMPETITIONS

Competitions vary in many different ways. They can be indoor or outdoor, which often makes a lot of difference, because outdoor competitions could involve the natural elements, such as wind and rain. They can even take place in a completely different medium, such as in the air or underwater. Obviously, all this drastically affects the design of your robot.

In some competitions, robots are supposed to be entirely unmanned ("autonomous"), while in others one can keep control over them via remote control ("teleoperated"). There can also be a combination of the two—typically robots start out on their own for a designated number of seconds, and once that period expires, users can control them.

Essentially, a competition centers on the nature of the task the robot is expected to do, and this is the single most important factor that will fundamentally affect the design. Sometimes the focus can be on locomotion, speed, and pathfinding skills, such as in the previously mentioned DARPA competition. Other times, it can concentrate more on swimming and hovering. Other competitions focus on manipulations, and the objective relates more to precision than speed and locomotion—in this case, the design of the arm/grabbing device is crucial.

Apart from these two major categories, there are many other types of competitions, some quite funny and sometimes bizarre. RoboCup pits robots against one another in a soccerplaying competition, for instance. RoboGames involve a variety of challenges mimicking the human Olympics, some involving wrestling, jumping, and other tasks. More exotic competitions are emerging by the day.

Robots play football (soccer) at the 10th International RoboCup Open in April 2015, which took place in Tehran, Iran. Enthusiasm for robot contests is a growing worldwide phenomenon.

DO YOUR HOMEWORK

Once the choices are narrowed down to a few candidates, it is time to look deeper into competition history. Look at the competitions that attracted attention, and examine past winners and competitors. Is the competition established, and will it be around this year or next? What did some of the previous designs consist of, especially the winners? What did the robots do? Is this something that can be matched or bettered? Would accomplishing this be within your team's budgetary constraints and expertise levels?

Finally, one must determine if one has the drive to win that competition. Is it exciting? Is it worth months of work, or longer, cooperating as a team, solving problem after problem, just for the competition and a chance to win it? If so, the next step is creating a solid team.

CHAPTER TWO

BUILD A TEAM

O ne of the most important aids in your quest to build competition-ready robots is a mentor. A mentor is any experienced, and often older and established, person who is a professional and/or veteran of his or her field who counsels younger enthusiasts and students, giving them encouragement, pointers and tips, and other guidance. The benefit of experience—especially those who know their way around robotics competitions—cannot be overstated.

In a school, the mentor will typically be a teacher, professor, or some other faculty member or administrator who has the expertise and the authority to have his or her advice considered, respected, and accepted. It is best if the mentor has had some direct experience not only with building robots, but also with attending, and ideally winning, robot competitions. The role of the mentor is most important when things are not running smoothly and problems are encountered.

PICKING MEMBERS—AND SKILL SETS

One thing that makes a great team is a group of people who have diverse skills that complement each other. In practice, this

Team members work together on their robot during the 14th Annual New York City FIRST Robotics Competition, held at the Javits Center in April 2014.

means that people are not alike, and one member has skills others lack, and vice versa.

Obviously, all team members need to share the same dedication, discipline, and desire to achieve the goal. But having a well-rounded group will tend to ensure that the group as a whole can leverage certain skills and resources. Some of these are:

- Experience: A history in participating in robot competitions and building robots in general is key. If someone on the team has been through the process before, his or her experience

TOOLS, AND A PLACE TO USE THEM

Access to equipment, materials, and space is not a skill, exactly, but is definitely important in competition planning. Some components can be hard to find, so being able to readily acquire them saves a lot of time and trouble. Access to convenient space for assembly and proper testing is also important and should not be underestimated. It is easy to believe you will easily find a space in which to work at least once a week and far more often in the lead-up to a competition. But be sure to secure a work space ahead of time, whether it is a shop area of your school or a team member's garage or similar space. Make sure to invest in the proper (and legal) safety equipment and measures. Consult with your mentor, faculty advisor, or a handy parent or relative at the very least to make sure you are not doing anything to put yourself, friends, family, or neighbors at risk.

will be very valuable, especially if the mentor won't be able to provide it full time.

- Leadership: The ability to assume responsibility and lead the team forward, maintain discipline, and adhere to the schedule will help whip the group into shape and give team members a sense of purpose.
- Engineering skills: An understanding of the underlying science is also essential. Engineering skills are the foundation

of a robot-building team. They include having a handle on hard science, creative problem solving, and design sense. One or more team members should know how to judge component requirements, figure out the feasibility of construction, and perform similar assessments.

- Practical skills: Working with different materials and components and construction-related skills (such as soldering, welding, etc.) are also extremely helpful.
- Programming: Experience in programming the microcontroller and general proficiency in the programming languages used is necessary.

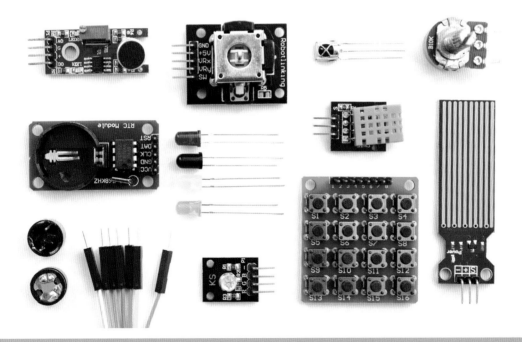

For robotics enthusiasts, shopping around for both new and repurposed parts, and then implementing them, can be an exciting and interesting hobby in and of itself.

- Graphic design skills: Some groups, such as US FIRST, work with community outreach. A member with graphic design skills would be able to design materials to hand out at competitions or otherwise promote the team.

Optimal team size will vary depending on the competition, but as a rule of thumb anywhere from three to ten members is a good bet, allowing for enough diversity but not needing complicated management. A dozen or more members becomes a more unwieldy organization where a stricter division of labor is appropriate and where strong specializations become more common.

MAKING A SCHEDULE

The timeline for the project will depend on when the competition is and how much time can be allocated per week to work on it. What can easily take newcomers to robot building by surprise is how often and how quickly one can fall behind schedule. There are numerous potential stumbling blocks to your team's success. A necessary component is three weeks late, or a team member goes on a vacation or drops out. Programming the robot to do a basic, simple function takes three weeks instead of two hours.

If some of these occur and are not planned and accounted for, you find yourself in a situation all too familiar to competition teams. One or more of the following usually happens: more and more time is allocated to the project; other projects or responsibilities in life suffer as a consequence; the team does last-minute "hacking," hoping things will miraculously work; or the team drops functionalities and focuses on what can be done in the time remaining. Or the team just gives up.

This can be avoided by adhering to the philosophy of American statesman and inventor Benjamin Franklin, who famously said, "Fail to prepare, prepare to fail." In other words, as it applies to a project like devising and preparing robots for competition: allow time for things to go wrong. Allow, for instance, every fourth team session as optional in case it is needed. That way it is still in the calendar but can be skipped if unnecessary. Plan for the robot to be ready several weeks before the actual competition, and then do meticulous testing.

Remember: the robot does not need to be constructed to perform every imaginable task. It need not even perform all of the tasks required by the competition. It just needs to beat the other teams. Quite often challenges set forth at competitions end up being very demanding, and no team even comes close to accomplishing them. For example, in the nineteen years that the famous Aerial Robotics Competition (ARC) has been held, a team managed to complete all the tasks required only once.

In practice, this means that one should make a list of functionalities planned for the robot, and then sort that list, prioritizing the most important ones. Is it more important that the robot is fast or that it does not drop objects? Should the team work on the robot's ability to recognize shapes or enhance its body's sturdiness? Sometimes the choices are obvious, sometimes less so. One set of functionalities may depend on another, and in these cases it is even harder to prioritize.

Once the team is assembled and the schedule organized, it is time to turn to actually building the robot and getting it into competition-winning shape. The next two chapters are dedicated to this purpose.

CHAPTER THREE

DESIGN AND CONSTRUCT

B efore the team builds a robot, even a great one, that robot must first be designed. Beginners to robotics competitions may be forced by necessity to skimp on this aspect at times, depending on their real experience. In one's first or second contest, design may constitute as little as 5 percent of your total labor time. With experience, that percentage will increase. But the more detailed and well planned a design, the less work will be necessary down the line.

THE BASIC BUILDING BLOCKS

Do not reinvent the wheel when designing your robot. Yes, your team

The FIRST Robotics Challenge Team 1885, also known by the name Inspiring Leaders in Technology and Engineering (ILITE), of Haymarket, Virginia, is shown in competition.

is trying to win a competition, and yes, the robot needs to be better than a group of others. But this does not mean that the team needs to change already proven and tested concepts just to be authentic. If the rules must be broken, then they should be learned before being broken. More often than not, there is a reason people do things in a particular way. Here are some things that should not be experimented with:

SAFETY FIRST, ALWAYS

The skills necessary to turn design into reality are important to have. How the robot is built will of course affect its performance. But before doing potentially dangerous things around the robot, the team should be sure to know what it is doing and have proper adult supervision when necessary. Normally, the voltages with which the team will be working aren't life-threateningly high, but any dealings with electrical current can potentially be dangerous. The same goes for activities such as drilling, welding, brazing, cutting, and soldering. Even though using too much of them can be an indication of bad design, they are often quite necessary, so it is important to learn about them and become confident performing them sooner rather than later.

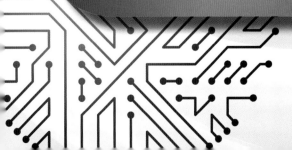

MATERIAL REQUIREMENT

For robots, aluminum or plastics are best. Each has their advantages and complement each other well. Aluminum is light, flexible, and highly resistant to corrosion and heat. Plastics are even lighter and very sturdy and durable. One would need serious reasons to use something like wood, steel, or some other nonstandard material. Almost always, the robot should be kept as light as possible and, in addition, its center of gravity kept low.

ACHIEVING LOCOMOTION

Ninety-nine percent of the time, a simple differential drive routine will work, and there is little or no need to fine-tune it. If the robot can go forward, backward, and turn, it is fine. For wheel surfaces, simple rubber materials that provide good friction are best. Wheel size will depend on the size of the robot, but generally the team will want to find the compromise between relatively fast locomotion and allowing enough time for the robot's sensors to detect the surroundings. For the castor, low-friction plastics are best.

A MOTOR OR SERVO?

Here is where the fact that a competition is in play will influence the decision process. Motors can spin freely in any direction for an unlimited amount of time. Servos have a limited range of motion, typically no more than 270°. However, servos are more sophisticated than motors, and it shows—they are much easier to control, and the sort of performance obtainable from them

Certain robotic components and building blocks can be bought in bulk by the team and kept for whenever they are needed, including commonly used items like fabricated tubes.

simply cannot be obtained from other motors. The problem with servos is that they are less intuitive and have specific voltage requirements. This means lower energy efficiency and a potentially bigger battery or shorter battery life, a fact that may or may not be relevant, depending on the competition.

POWER UP: BATTERY REQUIREMENTS

Again, this will directly depend on the type of competition being entered. Normally, battery life isn't a priority because batteries can be exchanged between attempts and because robots operate for a short time to begin with. If the team goes with NiMH or NiCad, it probably won't go wrong, providing the battery fits the robot's energy needs. Alkaline batteries are not recommended. They happen to be the most common, but they are very low capacity and are unable to provide energy bursts in short periods. For ease of access, it is best if the robot's battery is Velcro-attached and easy to remove and replace.

USING MICROCONTROLLERS

Another misconception is that if one is building a cutting-edge robot, an "old" microcontroller simply won't do. Nothing could be further from the truth. True, one won't get far with simple stamp-based controllers, but anything with decent programmability, such as Atmel's AVR, will not only do but will be capable of handling the most complicated routines sent its way. Again, it should be kept simple. A programmer (which uploads your program from the computer onto the chip) will be needed, unless the team is using a microcontroller that has an inbuilt programmer, such as Cerebellum. The latter option is highly recommended for convenience.

SHOP FOR SENSORS

Before planning for state-of-the-art sensors that will give the robot those coveted AI-like qualities, one should shop around. Sensors usually function on a binary scale—light/dark, fast/slow—and

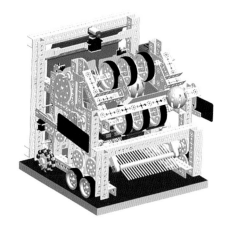

A machine is shown via the modeling provided by computer-aided design (CAD), which is a huge and convenient help in creating machines.

more often than not, they don't need to be sophisticated at all. A simple photoresistor can cost less than a dollar, and a pair of those can for instance be enough to give the robot the ability to avoid obstacles.

SOME ASSEMBLY REQUIRED

Keep the number of different types of screws and bolts used to a minimum. Use fewer parts, rather than more. Refrain from welding and soldering as much as possible (which should really be handled by an adult or professional, if performed). These are hard to undo if a mistake is made. All the heavy components of the robot should be located as close as possible to the ground, as it helps stability and saves battery. In the design phase especially, the robot should be kept as "open" as possible, with parts accessible and easily removable.

LOOKING FOR PARTS

The great advantage of following the above recommendations and keeping the basic components standard is that the team will be able to find them almost anywhere. Even if no one on the team could help find them, they can be readily located online on dedicated websites. One can make the basics for a competition-standard robot (that can later on be fine-tuned and developed) that would include all the above components for as low as $150 or even less without compromising on performance at all. Spend time and money on parts and design decisions that really matter and really need working on.

CHAPTER FOUR

BUILD YOUR ROBOT

The servo, the microcontroller, and the robot's sensors are some of the most integral parts of any robot to be entered into competition. Once team members have a good sense of the basics to these parts, they can then learn how to "break the rules" and modify them to improve or change the robot's functionality.

MODIFYING THE SERVO

The most common reason to modify the servo is to gain speed control. The normal servo doesn't rotate continuously because of an inbuilt potentiometer ("pot") that determines the angle at which the servo is. Working around this problem is one of the main ways of gaining flexibility and stability.

This is a kind of servomotor that hobbyists might use in radio-controlled model cars or other vehicles, as well as in many kinds of simple robots.

To achieve this, one will need to open up the servo and remove the safehorn from the output shaft, to keep the gears from falling out. Also, one will want to command the servo (via the microcontroller) to rotate to 0 degrees. Then unscrew the long screws in the corners and remove the pot, located under the largest gear. After that, the servo should be centered (back to 0 degrees) and the pot head rotated until the gears stop rotating. Then the pot should be glued back into position. After that, remove the pot slot from the gear—doing so will trick the servo into thinking it remains in a constant position. If all this is done correctly, and then the servo is reassembled, the robot will have achieved speed control, a very important feature for a number of tasks. Note, however, that not all robotics competitions allow for the modification of any of the motors, servos, or control systems.

THE SENSORS

Sensor understanding and control is the most important part of building a capable robot. Understanding of sensors varies considerably among enthusiasts. Most are able to use them and understand their importance but do not even begin to use their full potential. For a true competition contender, a robot needs to have more flexibility and angle control.

The key to achieving this is having an understanding of how sensor data is interpreted in mathematical form. Data should be gathered from the sensor and put into some visualization software. Any spreadsheet software will do just fine. Immediately, one can find some very interesting details about how the sensor works: mistakes it makes in calculating distance, certain ranges at which it works better or worse, and many other potentially useful things. These can later be used in fine-tuning the way the

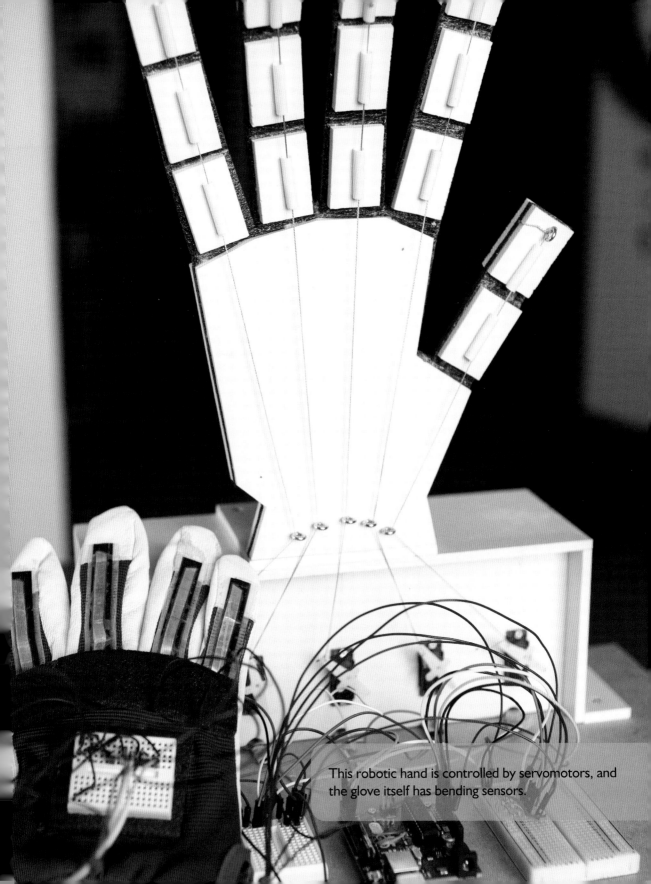

This robotic hand is controlled by servomotors, and the glove itself has bending sensors.

sensor is controlled, correcting for its errors, and achieving a very high degree of accuracy.

This is not to say that at some point finer or more sophisticated sensors won't be necessary, but one should first make sure current ones are being used to their full potential before moving on.

UNDERWATER WITH THE TORTUGA II

One of the biggest competitions for underwater robots was the Autonomous Underwater Vehicle Competition (AUVC). It was held annually and sponsored by the US Navy Office of Naval Research. For a time, the University of Florida had a stranglehold on the title, winning three times in a row in the years 2005-2007. However, the University of Maryland team managed to dethrone Florida in 2008 using its Tortuga II vessel.

The team understood the subtleties involved in the particular location where the competition was going to be held, which was San Diego, California. Visibility conditions underwater there vary widely, depending on the time of the day (morning clouds, strong direct sunlight during the day, and reddish glare in the evening), and the team thus focused most of its effort on designing and adapting its sensor/sonar/optical equipment and control software. On competition day, conditions indeed proved to be challenging, and no team had a stellar performance. But the Tortuga collected the most points, being the best of the robots despite not achieving all the competition goals.

HEART AND SOUL: THE MICROCONTROLLER

The microcontroller is the heart and soul of the robot. Grasping what is happening inside it, and how it affects the other components and their performance, is among the first advanced robot construction concepts that one will need to internalize. Knowledge of microcontroller workings will help beginner roboticist improve their designs, as well as streamline their building processes.

Your team will probably want to become familiar with some of the more basic algorithms, such as differential drive, line following, PID control, and working with timers, among others. At some point, the team should probably try building its own microcontroller, specifically an augmented microcontroller with more than just the chip on the integrated circuit. Components can be added, like LEDs, voltage regulators, capacitors, and so on. A developing board can be used, which is just a simple board with a few simple preexisting components that can be modified. It allows very quick testing of different configurations and designs. Knowledge about controlling analog (for sensors, for example) and digital ports (for LEDs and other components) is important.

PROGRAMMING

Unless the team wants to program in machine language, which is very impractical, C is the language of choice for programming microcontrollers for robots. Knowing what components can do and how they work together is a major part of the story, but it eventually does come down to writing the program code to control the robot's operation. The team will eventually have to have good understanding of C. They may not have to start writing programs from scratch, of course. Most of the functionalities necessary have already been programmed by someone and are readily available for free somewhere online.

C has been the language of choice for a long time, but some of the more sophisticated controllers, like National Instrument's cRIO, recently began using C++. The LEGO Mindstorms NXT brick can be programmed in a specially developed version of C, known as RobotC. Altogether, C and C++ are, nowadays, the closest to a standard language that robotics specialists can claim.

For projects of any size, and especially the more complex ones, taking care of code is essential, because the body of code created can quickly become too large to handle and keep track of. Fortunately, there are many services that are readily available free of charge for this purpose.

QUALITY TESTS

Already noted is the importance of allocating time for testing early on in the process. This becomes increasingly important as competition day approaches. There are two characteristics of good robot testing:

MODULARITY

Even the most simple robot eventually ends up being composed of hundreds of different components, many of which may fail to work properly. That is why it is incredibly important to test components from the early stages, and test them one by one, starting from the simplest individual ones and moving on to more complex subsystems.

This means one should test a sensor by first making sure the microcontroller is functioning well and that the input/output of

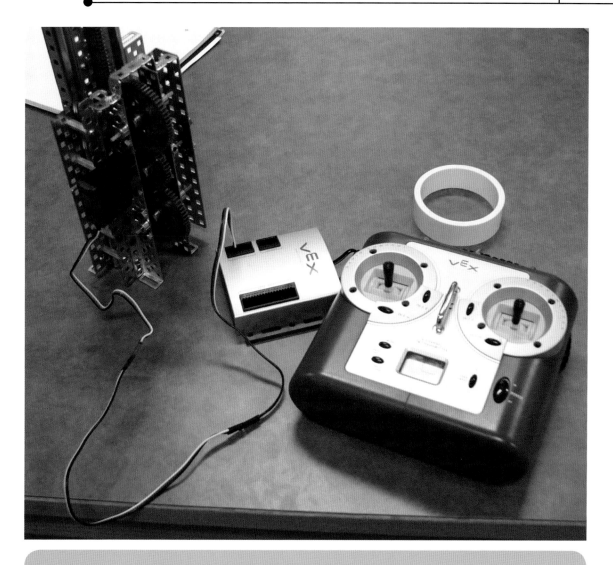

In this configuration that contended in the 2007 FIRST Tech Challenge Quad Quandary, controllers are connected to a robot with a lift mechanism; the controllers were programmed using the C programming language.

data is flowing properly. That way, if the sensor is not being used, the tester will know for sure that the problem is the result of the sensor malfunctioning, rather than some issue with the microcontroller or the communication channels.

It is generally best to start testing from the individual components of the microcontroller, on to the microcontroller as a whole, and then on to other peripheral systems and components. If this simple principle is overlooked, the poor builders end up in a position of simply having no way to narrow down the cause of a problem because of the lack of preliminary testing.

REALITY

However well the robot may be working, it is important to remember that one is preparing for a competition, which means the robot will need to perform a very particular task. To really test the robot, at the final stages of the testing schedule, the team should try the robot out on a course as close to the one in the competition as possible. Build a mock course if possible. Simulate other potential conditions, such as terrain and elements. Adhere to the timing restrictions for attempts, timing between attempts, battery recharging regulations, and any other piece of regulation that will be ruled on at the competition. That way the team will be so prepared that running the competition course will feel like just another test, with great performance and no surprises.

CHAPTER FIVE

GO HEAD-TO-HEAD

All the preparation and hard work of the weeks or even months preceding all lead up to the big day of the competition. A well-designed and constructed robot that is properly tested will stand a fighting chance of beating its competitors.

GETTING READY

Teams need to check their robot in, often referred to as check-in and inspections, and it needs to be tested to make sure it is compliant with the competition's restrictions. This is not the time to be finding out about those restrictions, so of course the robot will have been built with the competition format, limitations, and allowed parts in mind. Some competitions do allow some last-minute leeway when it comes to not-so-important parts (screws, some materials, etc.), but others are stricter, and if guidelines are not followed to the letter, the robot will be disqualified.

Meeting other contestants and the organizers is fun, but this is about winning, so the team will want to examine the course

A judge examines a competition robot closely. Many judges are former contestants themselves and might be teachers or work in robot development.

and see whether it can and should make some last minute modifications on the robot. Do this only if sure of what is being done—there is no time for testing now. This is why the team spent all this that time testing the robot in different configurations and setups—to limit the potential for surprises.

Depending on the competition, the robot will be allowed anywhere from one to more than five runs to complete the task. Usually it is more than one—judges understand that there is a chance component involved and wish to give the best robots

A TEAM EFFORT: WILDSTANG

The team that won the 2009 FIRST Robotics Competition is called WildStang and is a collaborative effort of students from Rolling Meadows and Wheeling High Schools and mentors from Motorola in Schaumburg, Illinois. The team has been competing in robotics competitions for more than fifteen years, and this experience has been transferred from generation to generation as students graduated and new ones came in.

The 2009 FIRST challenge was created to honor the fortieth anniversary of the moon landing and took place on a low-friction surface that made it difficult for robots to maneuver and served to mimic the low-gravity conditions found on the moon. The team members won by focusing on the basics—they discovered early on that maneuverability, control, and achieving friction were going to be key to winning and consequently focused most of their design efforts on creating a follower wheel system and a system for traction control, which made their robot's locomotion superior to that of other contestants.

On competition day, their robot simply outmaneuvered the others; other robots had superior moon rock collection abilities and more streamlined design but just could not compete with WildStang's control. They won the competition by understanding what the core problem was going to be and addressing it. WildStang also went on to win second place in 2011.

the opportunity to shine. Nobody wants the nightmare scenario where months of hard work are destroyed by a suddenly malfunctioning battery on the only run. Typically, the best run is the one that counts, and the team should look at what is happening —how the robot is doing and how the competition is performing. Adjustments should be made if necessary.

Audience members and participating teams check out the robots during the regional FIRST Competition at the San Diego Sports Arena in March 2009, a contest geared toward high school teams.

TRIAL, ERROR, AND IMPROVEMENT

Regardless of whether the robot wins or does not win, the team will feel that it just can't wait to go to the next competition. The excitement and the sense of fulfillment in seeing the effort finally resulting in a smart, well-running robot is hard to describe—it needs to be felt. Still, while now is definitely the time to relax and celebrate a little, one also needs to look back at the entire process and reflect. Be honest. Think of things that were done right and also of those that could have been done better. Think of the timeline—how did the team do on following the schedule? What

A winning student holds a trophy while examining the national standings in the FIRST Robotics Challenge after competition has concluded in St. Anthony, Minnesota, in March 2010.

can be learned for the future? How did the team perform? Did it lack skills in any department? Was the mentor helpful? Were there problems finding parts, and did the robot stay within the proposed budget? All of the above need to be considered if one is to learn from the experience and make sure the next attempt at winning a robot competition is even more successful.

Naturally, the feeling of winning even a small-scale or regional competition can be a thrilling one. And even the most seemingly inconsequential loss can hurt deep down. But there are things to learn from each experience. Few champions have remained undefeated their whole careers. Work hard and you and your team will have your chance and your time in the spotlight. But appreciate the process, too, and the friendship, teamwork, mentoring, and connections to be made. Enjoy, most of all, the sheer joy of creating and fielding a robot in competition.

GLOSSARY

AVR A modified single-chip 8-bit microcontroller developed by Atmel in 1996. It is very common in robots today because of its simplicity of use and programmability.

battery The power source for the robot. It is not different from batteries used for other uses and not very customizable; needs to match its purpose.

C The most common programming language used in robotics and more practical than machine code. Sometimes the more advanced C++ is used.

CAD Refers to computer-aided design software, such as Autocad, which is extremely helpful for the professional design of successful, working robots.

capacitor The component used to store electrons (power), useful for providing energy bursts, which batteries are not capable of.

differential drive The simplest locomotion mechanism.

expected forces Forces expected to be applied on particular parts of the robot (joints, components) during the robot's operation and especially during some high-stress tasks and movements.

LED Stands for light-emitting diode, a common type of light source used in robotics and other electronics.

line following An algorithm that makes a robot's movement dependent on a pre-designated line.

microcontroller A chip used to receive feedback and send instructions to a robot's components.

modularity A testing methodology that focuses on testing individual components first, then moving on to larger subsystems and eventually the entire robot.

motor A machine that uses electrical energy and produces mechanical energy.

pathfinding The act of discovering a route, or the best/quickest route between two positions.

photoresistor A type of resistor whose resistance decreases with increasing light density.

PID controller Short for proportional integral derivative controller, it denotes any controller that has built-in control loop feedback mechanisms.

pot Short for potentiometer, a part of a servomotor; also called a "variable resistor."

power requirements The voltage and power requirements of the robot and its individual components.

sensor Any device used for detecting other objects and calculating distances.

servo A type of motor that has built-in gearing and feedback correction for greater control.

voltage regulator A component commonly found on an augmented microcontroller, used to stabilize voltage input.

FIRST Robotics Competitions
200 Bedford Street
Manchester, NH 03101
(800) 871-8326
Website: https://www.firstinspires.org
Twitter: @FIRSTweets
FIRST Robotics Competitions are among the most well known of
their kind nationwide and internationally, and their websites
provides information about past challenges, upcoming contests, and scholarship opportunities.

IEEE Robotics and Automation Society
445 Hoes Lane
Piscataway, NJ 08854
(732) 562-3906
Website: http://www.ieee-ras.org
Twitter: @ieeeras
A national society, the Robotics and Automation Society is part
of the Institute of Electrical and Electronic Engineers (IEEE)
and offers professional and student chapters that focus on
advancing innovation, education, and research dealing with
robotics and automation.

Robotics Society of Southern California (RSSC)
800 North State College Boulevard
Fullerton, CA 92831
Website: http://www.rssc.org
Facebook: @roboticssocietyofsoutherncalifornia
YouTube: https://www.youtube.com/user/RSSCRobotics
The RSSC organizes its own competition each year and is one of
the biggest societies by membership in the United States.

Seattle Robotics Society
PO Box 1714
Duvall, WA 98019-1714
Website: http://www.seattlerobotics.org
A nonprofit enthusiasts' group whose members include amateurs and professionals, high school students, and college professors, the Seattle Robotics Society offers newcomers to robotics online chat sessions and information on getting started with projects.

Western Canadian Robotics Society
c/o The Hangar Flight Museum
4629 McCall Way NE
Calgary, AB T2E 8A5
Canada
Website: http://www.robotgames.com
Facebook: @WCRS.YYC
The Western Canadian Robotics Society is dedicated to the advancement of "personal robotics" and organizing robotics competitions in Western Canada.

WEBSITES

Due to the changing nature of internet links, Rosen Publishing has developed an online list of websites related to the subject of this book. This site is updated regularly. Please use this link to access the list:

http://www.rosenlinks.com/HOR/Build

FOR FURTHER READING

Brasch, Nicolas. *Robots and Artificial Intelligence*. Mankato, MN: Smart Apple Media, 2011.

Freedman, Jeri, and Margaux Baum. *The History of Robots and Robotics* (Hands-on Robotics). New York, NY: Rosen Publishing, 2018.

Greek, Joe. *Artificial Intelligence* (Digital and Information Literacy). New York, NY: Rosen Publishing, 2018.

Hustad, Douglas. *Discover Robotics*. Minneapolis, MN: Lerner Publications, 2017.

La Bella, Laura. *The Future of Robotics* (Hands-on Robotics). New York, NY: Rosen Publishing, 2018.

Mara, Wil. *Robotics Engineers* (Cool STEAM Careers/21st Century Skills Library). Ann Arbor, MI: Cherry Lake Publishing, 2015.

Parker, Steve. *Robots in Science and Medicine*. Mankato, MN: Smart Apple Media, 2011.

Payment, Simone, and Margaux Baum. *Building a Career in Robotics* (Hands-on Robotics). New York, NY: Rosen Publishing, 2018.

Peppas, Lynn. *Robotics*. New York, NY: Crabtree Publishing, 2015.

Ryan, Peter K. *Powering Up a Career in Robotics* (Preparing for Tomorrow's Careers). New York, NY: Rosen Publishing, 2015.

Spilsbury, Louise, and Richard Spilsbury. *Robotics*. New York, NY: Gareth Stevens Publishing, 2017.

BIBLIOGRAPHY

Appin Knowledge Solutions. *Robotics*. Hingham, MA: Infinity Science Press, 2007.

Bekey, George A. *Autonomous Robots: From Biological Inspiration To Implementation And Control*. Cambridge, MA: MIT Press, 2005.

Choset, Howie M. *Principles Of Robot Motion: Theory, Algorithms, And Implementation*. Cambridge, MA: MIT Press, 2005.

Hawkins, Jeff; Blakesless, Sandra. *On Intelligence*. New York, NY: Times Books, 2004.

Huang, Han-Way. *PIC Microcontroller: An Introduction To Software And Hardware Interfacing*. Clifton Park, NY: Thomson/Delmar Learning, 2005.

Jazar, Reza N. *Theory Of Applied Robotics: Kinematics, Dynamics, And Control*. New York: Springer, 2007.

Mataric, Maja J. *The Robotics Primer*. Cambridge, MA: MIT Press, 2007.

Perdue, David J. *The Unofficial LEGO Mindstorms Nxt Inventor's Guide*. San Francisco, CA: No Starch Press, 2008.

Platt, Charles. Make: *Electronics: Learning By Discovery*. Sebastopol, CA: O'Reilly, 2009.

Predko, Michael. *123 Robotics Experiments For The Evil Genius*. New York, NY: McGraw-Hill, 2004.

Siciliano, Bruno. *Robotics: Modeling, Planning And Control*. London, United Kingdom: Springer, 2009.

Siciliano, Bruno, ed., and Oussama Khatib. *Springer Handbook of Robotics*. Berlin, Germany: Springer, 2008.

Siegwart, Roland, and Illah Reza Nourbakhsh. *Introduction to Autonomous Mobile Robots*. Cambridge, MA: MIT Press, 2004.

Singer, P.W. *Wired for War: The Robotics Revolution and Conflict in the Twenty-First Century*. New York, NY: Penguin Press, 2009.

Spong, Mark W., Seth Hutchinson, and M. Vidyasagar. *Robot Modeling and Control*. Hoboken, NJ: John Wiley & Sons, 2006.

St. Amour, Madeline. "Messalonskee High Students to Compete Overseas in China Robotics Competition." *Kennebec Journal & Morning Sentinel,* May 25, 2017. http://www.centralmaine .com/2017/05/25/messalonskee-high-students-to-compete -in-china-robotics-competition.

Thrun, Sebastian, Wolfram Burgard, and Dieter Fox. *Probabilistic Robotics*. Cambridge, MA: MIT Press, 2005.

INDEX

A

Aerial Robotics Competition, 18
Autonomous Underwater Vehicle
    Competition, 28
AVR, 23

B

Baxter Bomb Squad (Mountain
    Home High School), 9

C

C, 29–30
C++, 30

F

For Inspiration and Recognition in
    Science and Technology (FIRST),
    9, 35

L

LEGO Mindstorms NXT, 30

M

microcontrollers, 23, 29
modularity, 30–32
motors, 21

P

photoresistors, 24
potentiometer (pot), 25, 26

R

RoboCup, 11
RoboGames, 11
RobotC, 30
robotics competitions
    benefits of participating, 6
    checking robot in to contest, 33
    examining contest course, 33–34
    growth in popularity, 4
    mentors, importance of, 13
    multiple runs, 34, 36
    researching, importance of, 7, 12
    skills needed, 4–5
    trial, error, and improvement, 37–38
    variety/categories, 10–11
robotics competitions, preparing for
    budget, 9–10
    tasks robot needs to perform,
        10–11, 18
    time/planning, 8, 17–18
    winning, 9
robotics competitions, team building
    access to resources, 15
    optimal team size, 17
    skill sets, 13–17
robots, building
    finding parts, 24
    microcontroller, modifying, 29
    programming, 29–30
    safety, importance of, 20
    sensors, modifying, 26, 28
    servos, modifying, 25–26
robots, designing
    autonomous vs. teleoperated, 10

batteries, 22–23
locomotion, 21
materials, 21
microcontroller, 23
motor vs. servo, 21–22
sensors, 23–24
using fewer parts, 24
robots, quality testing
component by component, 30–32
mock course, 32

S

science, technology, engineering,
and math (STEM), 4
sensors, 23–24, 26, 28
servos, 21–22, 25–26

T

Tortuga II (University of Maryland),
28

W

WildStang, 35

ABOUT THE AUTHORS

Margaux Baum is a writer and editor from New York with many technology-related credits for young adult readers.

Joel Chaffee is a writer of nonfiction and fiction currently at Columbia University. His academic career includes studies in history, literature, cinema/filmmaking, and writing. A wonder at the natural world caused him to further pursue knowledge in the fields of science, mathematics, and even robots.

PHOTO CREDITS